For Pou

—S. F.-D.

POEMS IN THIS COLLECTION FIRST APPEARED IN THE FOLLOWING BOOKS:

Always Wondering (HarperCollins, 1991): MY CHRISTMAS TREE (orig. CHRISTMAS TREE)

Feathered Ones and Furry (New York: Crowell, 1971): MERRY CHRISTMAS

The House of a Mouse (New York: Harper & Row, 1988): FIRST SNOW; SNOW STITCHES

In One Door and Out the Other (New York: Crowell, 1969): CHRISTMAS TREE; WINTER

Out in the Dark and Daylight (New York: Harper & Row, 1980): BEFORE CHRISTMAS; CHRISTMAS IN THE COUNTRY; FALL WIND; FROSTY WINDOW; SPARKLY SNOW; WINTER STARS

Set the Stage for Christmas (Evanston, IL: Row, Peterson, 1948): OF COURSE THERE IS A SANTA CLAUS

That's Why (New York: T. Nelson & Sons, 1946): DECEMBER

Up the Windy Hill (New York: Abelard Press, 1953): DO RABBITS HAVE CHRISTMAS?

Henry Holt and Company, LLC, *Publishers since 1866*

175 Fifth Avenue, New York, New York 10010

www.henryholtchildrensbooks.com

Henry Holt® is a registered trademark of Henry Holt and Company, LLC.

Compilation copyright © 2007 by the Boulder Public Library Foundation, Inc.

Illustrations copyright © 2007 by Sarah Fox-Davies

All rights reserved. Distributed in Canada by H. B. Fenn and Company Ltd.

Library of Congress Cataloging-in-Publication Data

Fisher, Aileen Lucia, 1906–2002

Do rabbits have christmas? / poems by Aileen Fisher; illustrated by Sarah Fox-Davies.—1st ed.

p. cm.

ISBN-13: 978-0-8050-7491-8 / ISBN-10: 0-8050-7491-0

I. Fox-Davies, Sarah, ill. II. Title.

PS3511.I7294D6 2007 811'.52—dc22 2006030504

First Edition—2007 / Designed by Amelia May Anderson

Printed in China on acid-free paper. ∞

1 3 5 7 9 10 8 6 4 2

Do Rabbits Have Christmas?

poems by *Aileen Fisher*

illustrated by *Sarah Fox-Davies*

HENRY HOLT AND COMPANY ★ NEW YORK

A NOTE TO READERS

It's very early in the morning on Bainbridge Island in the state of Washington, and I am sitting in front of my beloved, but continually mystifying, laptop. The month is August and some fluffy white clouds are stretched out at treetop height, discussing the brilliant sunrise and the developing day.

It is nowhere near Christmas.

Nevertheless...I have just read a collection of poems by Aileen Fisher. Lines full of snow and mice and wrapping paper. Lines full of words and pictures that evoke past and future Christmases for all of us present. And when I lift my head from the computer screen in front of me and look out to see the currents start to eddy across Agate Pass, I see, instead, snow falling. These poems do what poems should do: They take you someplace wonderful, someplace else. Someplace where the world is white "when we go stomping out" and "footprints full of diamonds / follow us about." I have always loved this magical ability that words have, that books have. The ability to take us anywhere.

Aileen Fisher died in 2002. But read her words, because they remain very much alive. And they give you—and me—the gift of a white and thoroughly Merry Christmas.

—Karla Kuskin

Fall Wind

Everything is on the run—
willows swishing in the sun,
branches full of dip and sway,
falling leaves that race away,
pine trees tossing on the hill—
nothing's quiet, nothing's still,
all the sky is full of song:
"Winter's coming. Won't be long."

First Snow

When autumn stills
the crickets
and yellow leaves turn brown,
I wonder what
a Mouseling thinks
as snow starts falling down,
and petal
after petal
goes trickling down his nose
and there's
a strange, cold tickle
between his slender toes?

Snow Stitches

Who's the one
in winter's house
who likes to stitch and sew?

Around the meadow's
new white blouse
some dainty footprints go.

No, not a hare.
No, not a grouse.
But just a plucky little Mouse . . .

That's the one
whose footprints show
like stitches in the new white snow.

December

I like days
with a snow-white collar,
and nights when the moon
is a silver dollar,
and hills are filled
with eiderdown stuffing
and your breath makes smoke
like an engine puffing.

I like days
when feathers are snowing,
and all the eaves
have petticoats showing,
and the air is cold
and the wires are humming,
but you feel all warm . . .
with Christmas coming.

Sparkly Snow

Last night the sky was reckless,
a reckless millionaire:
it threw down chips of diamonds
and strewed them everywhere.
And on this bright cold morning
when we go stomping out
footprints full of diamonds
follow us about.

Before Christmas

We sing, and plan,
and watch the date,
and write some cards . . .
and wait and wait.

We look for presents
at the store
and make some, too . . .
and wait some more.

We wrap our gifts
and tie them straight,
and frost some cookies
on a plate,
and buy a tree
to decorate,
but most of all
we wait . . . and wait.

Christmas Tree

My kitten thinks
the Christmas tree
is more than something
just to see.

She taps the balls
of green and red,
and swings the tinsel
overhead,

And rings the bells,
and starts to purr
as if we'd trimmed it
all for her.

Frosty Window

The frosted window
shows tall white ferns,
and trees, and rivers
with twists and turns,
and strange white forests
with flowers of ice . . .
wish I could *walk*
in a place that nice.

My Christmas Tree

I'll find me a spruce
in the cold white wood
with wide green boughs
and a snowy hood.

I'll pin on a star
with five gold spurs
to mark my spruce
from the pines and firs.

I'll make me a score
of suet balls
to tie to my spruce
when the cold dusk falls.

And I'll hear next day
from the sheltering trees
the Christmas carols
of the chickadees.

Of Course There Is a Santa Claus

Of course there is a Santa Claus!
You may not see him driving
his little reindeer through the sky
or hear him on arriving,
but he is there, on Christmas Eve,
with jolly secrets up his sleeve.

Of course there is a Santa Claus!
You may not see him climbing
inside a chimney Christmas Eve
when midnight bells are chiming,
but he is there that magic night,
although you never catch him—quite.

Of course there is a Santa Claus!
You may not hear him chuckle
or see his red and bulging coat
with flashing belt and buckle,
but he is there . . . in every heart
where giving plays a merry part!

Christmas in the Country

Run, little wild ones,
over the snow,
peek through the trees
where yourselves won't show,
look at the lights
on our Christmas tree,
brighter than any
stars you'll see!

Do Rabbits Have Christmas?

Do rabbits have Christmas,
I wonder, I wonder?

They have little spruces
to celebrate under,
where snow has made pompons
with silvery handles,
and frost has made tinsel
and icicle candles.

Do rabbits have presents,
I wonder, I wonder?

They have little fir trees
to celebrate under.
But do they have secrets
and smiles on their faces?
Let's go put some carrots
in rabbit-y places!

Merry Christmas

I saw on the snow
when I tried my skis
the track of a mouse
beside some trees.
Before he tunneled
to reach his house
he wrote "Merry Christmas"
in white, in mouse.

Winter Stars

Winter is the time for stars;
for hours and hours they shine
on sparkly fields and icy ponds
and snowy roofs, like mine.

They shine before its dinnertime,
and on till breakfast's due . . .
I think they must get very tired
before the winter's through.

Winter

Winter doesn't have picnics
under the bright green leaves,

But winter has daggers of icicles
that dangle from the eaves.

Winter doesn't have swimming,
or camping, or balls to bat,

But winter has Christmas, and nothing,
nothing is better than that.